Was Mary Queen of Scots a martyr or a monster? She lived in the midst of political and religious intrigue; her life was beset with foul plots and murders. Yet, after her execution, her reputation for courage and beauty quickly grew into a romantic legend.

The reign of Scotland's most famous monarch was full of crisis and drama. When only seven days old she became Queen of a violently-divided Scotland. Betrothed at the age of five to the Dauphin Francis, she spent thirteen years in France, the darling of the luxurious French court. On her return home she became the focus of plots and rebellions against her cousin, Elizabeth I.

Then came imprisonment and enforced abdication, an exciting escape and an attempt to regain her throne. On fleeing to England she was again imprisoned, this time by Elizabeth I. For eighteen years she was suspected of plotting against the English Queen. In October 1586 she was accused and tried for treason. Finally she was, in her own words, "executed like a criminal", though "innocent of any crime".

Was she really innocent, a victim of circumstance? Or were her enemies justified in their accusations? With the help of contemporary documents and illustrations, Alan Bold examines her life and the facts of the case against her, providing an essential aid to the study of Tudor and Stuart history.

Mary
Queen of Scots

Alan Bold

WAYLAND PUBLISHERS

More Wayland Kings and Queens

Alfred the Great	Jennifer Westwood
Henry VIII	David Fletcher
Elizabeth I	Alan Kendall
James I	David Walter
Charles I	Hugh Purcell
Charles II	Michael Gibson
Queen Victoria	Richard Garrett
Louis XIV	Christopher Martin
Napoleon	Stephen Pratt
Kaiser Bill	Richard Garrett
Peter the Great	Michael Gibson
Catherine the Great	Miriam Kochan

Frontispiece Mary Queen of Scots. Is she looking back to France and her past happiness, or forward to Scotland?

SBN 85340 419 4

Copyright © 1977 by Wayland (Publishers) Ltd
First published in 1977 by Wayland (Publishers) Ltd,
49 Lansdowne Place, Hove, East Sussex BN3 1HS
Printed by Butler & Tanner Ltd, Frome and London

Contents

1 Fatherless Child

MARY STUART was only one week old when she became Queen of a newly defeated Scotland. Her father, James V, had sent ten thousand men to crush three thousand of Henry VIII's Englishmen at the battle of Solway Moss, but to the Scottish King's despair he lost the battle and, with it, his pride. Although he was only thirty, he welcomed death; nothing could revive his spirits. When he heard that his wife had given birth to a daughter, his sad comment was: "It came with a lass, it will pass with a lass." The Stewarts had become Scotland's royal family through marriage with a daughter of Robert the Bruce, and he thought the day of the Stewarts would end with his daughter's beginning.

Mary was born on 8th December, 1542 at Linlithgow Palace, six days before the death of her father. Her clever mother, the Queen Dowager Mary of Guise (1515–60), needed all her wisdom to decide on a suitable partner for Mary. This was doubly important, for Mary was not only Queen of Scots but, as Margaret Tudor's granddaughter, she was next in line to the English throne after the children of Henry VIII.

Because of her Roman Catholic religion and French connections, Mary of Guise would have liked a marriage alliance that linked her daughter with Francis I of France. Scotland and France were old allies who had often combined to curb the power of England. Unfortunately, there were no suitable French princes available at the time. The leading Roman Catholic in Scotland, Cardinal David Beaton of St Andrews (1494–1546), formed his own plan. First he would persuade the new Governor (or Regent) of Scotland, the Earl of Arran (1515–75), to support Roman Catholic interests. Then

IACOBVS·5·D·GRA· REX·SCOTORVM

Above James V of Scotland, Mary's father. He was nicknamed "King of the commons" because he cared for his people and visited them in their homes.

Opposite Mary of Guise, Mary's French mother. Twice widowed by the age of twenty-seven, she had nearly as stormy a life as her daughter.

Above George Wishart, the Scottish martyr who inspired John Knox. A schoolteacher until he was charged twice with heresy, he was arrested and burned to death for preaching the Protestant doctrine.

"All men lamented that the realm was left without a male to succeed." *John Knox,* History of the Reformation in Scotland *1586.*

he would arrange a marriage between Arran's son James and Mary Queen of Scots. Cardinal Beaton was confident that he could control Arran and dictate to him on matters of religion.

So when Henry VIII (1491–1547) arranged by the Treaties of Greenwich of 1st July, 1543 to marry Mary to his five-year-old son Edward, Cardinal Beaton put his plan into action. He could hardly agree to an English marriage after Henry VIII had defied the Pope by marrying Anne Boleyn. Backed by seven thousand men, he took Mary from Linlithgow Palace to Stirling Castle, where she would be safe from the English. Then he received Arran into the Roman Catholic Church. Henry VIII's reaction was to begin his "rough wooing" of Mary. He unleashed England's armed might onto Scotland.

Although Scotland suffered agony at the hands of Henry VIII, the little Queen was never captured. Yet all her subjects did not support her in her hour of need. All over Europe there were men who wanted to reform the religion, and they would rather have died than live under the Catholic Church. In Scotland, where the Catholic Church owned about half the nation's wealth, the Reformers were led by George Wishart.

Infuriated by criticism of his religion, Cardinal Beaton had Wishart arrested and burned to death in St Andrews Castle in March 1546, while he watched. This was Beaton's last act of persecution, because three months later he himself was seized by supporters of Wishart, stabbed to death and displayed on the foretower of St Andrews Castle. The Reformers held the castle until Arran summoned the French fleet to remove and punish them.

In 1547, both Francis I of France and Henry VIII died. Even without their great King, the English proved strong enough to defeat Arran at the battle of Pinkie Cleugh. It seemed likely that the English would overrun Scotland, so the infant Queen of Scots was taken from Stirling Castle to the safety of Inchmahome island. To this day there is a tree, a bower and a garden named

Above Stirling Castle, where Mary was crowned Queen of the Scots in 1543. It was her fortress home for part of her early life.

after Mary on Inchmahome. It is doubtful if a four-year-old royal fugitive would have had the time to do so much gardening in three weeks, but Inchmahome remains part of the legend of Mary Queen of Scots.

Mary of Guise now felt threatened on two counts: by the English victors of Pinkie Cleugh, and by the Scottish opponents of the Catholic Church. With Cardinal Beaton murdered and Governor Arran discredited for cowardly conduct at Pinkie Cleugh, Mary of Guise was in a position to make her own decisions. She was delighted when the new French King Henry II proposed marriage between the Queen of Scots and his son the Dauphin Francis (1544–60). It was the French alliance she had always wanted, and the Scottish Parliament approved it on 7th July, 1548. The next month, the five-year-old Queen of Scots left Dumbarton for France, aboard Henry II's royal galley. Among her companions were four young noble ladies of her own age, Mary Fleming, Mary Seaton, Mary Beaton and Mary Livingstone. With these four Maries (as maids-of-honour were then known in Scotland), she sailed to her future in France. The four Maries are remembered as the "pretty maids all in a row" of the nursery rhyme. Mary's own destiny was to be rather more stormy.

> "Just as we see, half rosy and
>   half white
> Dawn and the Morning Star
>   dispel the night
> In beauty thus beyond compare
>   impearled
> The Queen of Scotland rises on
>   the world." *Pierre de Ronsard*
> *(1524–85).*

9

2 A French Education

MARY WAS TO SPEND the next thirteen years of her life in France. Indeed at the time of her arrival no one seriously thought she would ever see Scotland again. As the future Queen, she was taught to think of France as her own country, and from the beginning she was the darling of the French court. Henry II was delighted with her, while Mary's grandmother Antoinette of Guise wrote: "She will be a beautiful girl, for her complexion is fine and clear, the skin white, the lower part of the face very pretty, the eyes are small and rather deep set, the face rather long, she is graceful and not shy, and on the whole we may be well contented with her."

When Mary first arrived in France she could speak only English, and she must have been confused after life at Stirling Castle, the sudden flight to the island abbey and the long sea voyage. But at last she had a home. Her Guise uncles were among the most powerful men in France, especially Duke Francis and Cardinal Charles. They looked after their niece because she guaranteed them a place at the French court. Mary grew up with her future husband, the Dauphin Francis, in beautiful palaces like Fontainebleau, and she learned French so well that for the rest of her life she wrote and thought in French, and signed her name "Marie" and not "Mary".

Mary took lessons in Italian, Latin and Greek, but her education was not confined to books. French court life was gay and graceful, so Mary also learned to draw, play the lute and to sing and dance. Even as a child her talent at dancing was exceptional. She went every

> **"The little Queen of Scots is the most perfect child that I have ever seen."** *Henry II of France.*

Opposite "The Convent Garden—France" by Robert Herdman. For thirteen years Mary enjoyed the pleasant and cultured life of the French court. Her companions, the four Maries, had travelled with her from Scotland as young children.

Right Three hundred Protestants were burned at the stake during the last three years of Mary I's reign. This engraving from the Rev Dr Southwell's *New Book of Martyrs* commemorates the death of eleven men and two women at Stratford in Essex in 1556.

day to Mass and became a devout Roman Catholic. Everything was perfect for her in the rich shimmering world that was the French court. When Mary of Guise came to visit her in 1550, she was happy with her daughter's progress. After a year she returned to Scotland, and Mary never saw her mother again.

Scotland was still officially a Roman Catholic country. Now Protestant England was brutally returned to the Catholic fold. When young Edward VI of England died in 1553, his sister restored the Catholic religion with such force that she earned the nickname of "Bloody Mary" Tudor (1516–58). In four years three

hundred Protestants died at the stake. In 1554, Mary of Guise became Regent of Scotland in place of Arran, who contented himself with accepting the French Dukedom of Châtelherault. Although much less bloodthirsty than "Bloody Mary" Tudor, Mary of Guise also wanted to see the defeat of the Protestants. As she had her Regency, the support of the Pope, and her Guise relations in France, what did her Protestant enemies have?

First and most important, they had complete faith in themselves and in the teaching of the Swiss preacher John Calvin (1509–64). Calvin believed that the Roman Catholic Church was evil and corrupt, with its vast wealth and ceremony, glorifying the priests and the Pope at the expense of God. Above all he believed that Christ's sacrifice was made on behalf of "the elect", a select few born for salvation, and that others were doomed to eternal damnation. Calvin set up his own state in Geneva, and his ideas soon spread to France, where his followers were called Huguenots. But Scotland's John Knox (1505–72) was his most passionate follower. This peasant's son had spent nineteen months as a galley slave on a French ship for his part in the siege of St Andrews Castle. On release, he had gone to England as one of Edward VI's royal chaplains. When "Bloody Mary" came to the English throne, Knox wisely fled to Geneva to be with Calvin, still determined to destroy the rich and powerful Catholic Church.

Of these developments Mary knew next to nothing. They did not affect her life. Her position at the French court was pleasant. There was no reason to believe that the Huguenots could threaten the strength of the French throne. Mary had her four Maries, and her Dauphin, and her games to amuse her. Yet while Mary's life revolved around her forthcoming marriage to the Dauphin Francis, John Knox was in Geneva writing a book called *The First Blast of the Trumpet Against the Monstrous Regiment of Women*, in which he bluntly stated his view: "To promote a woman to bear rule, superiority, dominion, or empire above any realm, nation, or city, is repugnant to nature."

England had "Bloody Mary", Scotland had Mary of Guise. Now Mary was to join this "monstrous regiment" by becoming the wife of the future King of France. Scotland was only a memory, a poor country she could afford to forget. She did not imagine that she had already made enemies like the Dauphin's mother Catherine de Medici, who hated the House of Guise. Nor in her wildest dreams could she have imagined that life had the likes of John Knox in store for her.

15

3 The First Marriage

ON 24TH APRIL, 1558, Mary Queen of Scots married the Dauphin Francis, in the Cathedral of Notre Dame de Paris. She was fifteen years old and her husband a year younger. In her magnificent bejewelled wedding robe, Mary looked every inch a young queen, although white was an unusual choice for a wedding dress, as it was associated with royal mourning in France. Of course no one objected, and clearly there was no sadness in Mary's heart on that occasion. As Queen of Scots by birth and now future Queen of France by marriage, she must have felt that she deserved every word of praise that court poets like Pierre de Ronsard showered upon her, hymning her as a beauty beyond compare.

Only a few months after her marriage, a third kingdom seemed within her reach. "Bloody Mary" Tudor, wife of Philip II of Spain, died childless and the English throne passed to her unmarried half-sister Elizabeth (1533–1603), daughter of Henry VIII and his second wife Anne Boleyn. As the Pope had not recognized Henry VIII's divorce, Roman Catholics could not consider Elizabeth as proper heir to the English throne. To them Mary Queen of Scots had the better claim. So Henry II of France took this opportunity to proclaim his daughter-in-law Mary rightful Queen of England. When Mary began to use the title and arms of the Queen of England, however, Elizabeth I was not amused. What is more, she never forgave Mary.

It was not long before Mary's husband inherited his father's kingdom. Henry II died in July 1559, after

> "Lo! the potent hand of God from above sent unto us a wonderful and most joyful deliverance. For unhappy Francis, husband to our sovereign, suddenly perished of a rotten ear." *John Knox, History of the Reformation in Scotland, 1586.*

Overleaf A contemporary engraving of a Huguenot massacre in 1561.

Opposite The young King and Queen of France.

Above Elizabeth I, Queen of England from 1558–1603.

being stabbed in the eye and throat by a splinter from a lance in a friendly jousting match. The Dauphin was crowned King Francis II at Rheims two months later. This was a great triumph for the House of Guise, who felt they could control France by using their influence on Mary. However much Henry's widow, the Queen Dowager Catherine de Medici, resented the Guise family's power, she could do nothing about it as long as Mary was the wife of Francis II.

Mary had an opportunity to see what this power involved when the French court moved to Amboise, a medieval fortress, in March 1560. A group of Huguenots planned to take Francis II from the clutches of the House of Guise and establish a Protestant regime. When their attack came to grief on the walls of the fortress, revenge was swift and savage. Mary's Guise uncles watched the Huguenots publicly executed as an after-dinner amusement.

In the same year in Scotland, the Protestant rebels had more success. Calling themselves the Lords of the Congregation, the Scottish nobles were now well organized against Mary of Guise. They had the Duke of Châtelherault, the former Regent (now a Protestant again) as figurehead, William Maitland as political leader and John Knox as inspiration. Elizabeth I, still furious at Mary's claim to be Queen of England, sent English troops to help the Scottish nobles besiege Mary of Guise's French troops at Leith. Mary of Guise retired defeated to Edinburgh Castle, where she died from dropsy. The Protestants moved quickly. First, a Treaty of Edinburgh removed the French from Scotland and proclaimed Elizabeth, not Mary, as rightful Queen of England. Then the Scottish Parliament passed a Confession of Faith to establish the Protestant religion. Finally, a week later, Parliament abolished the authority of the Pope and prohibited the Mass.

Before the year 1560 was out, Mary suffered a second loss. Her sickly husband Francis II died of an inflammation of the ear, and the eighteen-year-old widow wrote a poem about her grief. In Geneva John Calvin did not shed any tears. On the contrary he rejoiced that "God who had pierced the father's eye, struck off the ear of his son." Catherine de Medici assumed control of France, demanding that Mary immediately return the French crown jewels. To her mother-in-law, Mary had always been a reminder of the House of Guise and its power, and now she was no longer welcome in France. The solution for Mary seemed to be to find a new husband. Her first thought was to marry Don Carlos, heir to Philip II's Spanish Empire, but the prejudiced Catherine de Medici, with her fear of the Guise family, persuaded Philip II against the marriage. Of course, Mary was still Queen of Scots, and her half-brother Lord James Stewart (1531–70), one of the Lords of the Congregation, came over to France to ask her home to Scotland. He assured her that she would be welcome, and that nobody would object to her observing her own religion in private, even though the country was now Protestant. Besides, he promised to guide and protect her personally. In the circumstances it was the best offer available.

So, in the company of her four Maries and her French companions, Mary left Calais in August 1561. For the second time in her life she was taking a journey into the unknown, for her momories of Scotland were by now misty. As she left France in tears she cried: "Goodbye my dear France, I think I shall never see you again." She was soon to have even more reason to shed her tears. And, as she suspected, she would never see France again.

Above right Mary aged seventeen. This portrait was engraved by W Bond from an enamel by H Bone, which in turn was painted after the original by Sir A More.

> "What formerly was pleasant to my eyes
> Now gives me pain
> The brightest day,
> To me, seems dark and obscure night.
> For the most exquisite delights
> I now have neither relish or desire." *Mary Queen of Scots on the death of Francis II in 1560.*

4 Return to Scotland

WHEN MARY ARRIVED at Leith, she wept again at the sight of the poor horses provided for her party. That, and the appalling weather, added up to a bad start. According to John Knox: "The mist was so thick and dark that scarcely might any man espy another the length of two pairs of boots." To the leader of the Scottish Reformation, this was a terrible omen—God's curse on the coming of a Catholic queen to a Protestant country. Mary, however, had come to claim a kingdom, and many Scotsmen were pleased to see her. She was cheered all the way from Leith to the Palace of Holyrood in Edinburgh.

Holyrood was hardly a grand enough home for someone accustomed to French court life, and Scotland itself must have seemed a grim prospect. It was a country of terrible poverty. Mary had just left a prosperous land of some twelve million people. Scotland in the sixteenth century had a population of only seven hundred thousand, almost all peasants living in hovels. Most towns were unwalled, most roads were useless, most farms were utterly primitive. What wealth there was had passed from the once-powerful Catholic Church into the hands of the Protestant nobles. To the disgust of John Knox, the lot of the peasant had hardly changed.

The country itself was divided. In the Lowlands based around Edinburgh, the Reformation was complete, and the Protestant nobles were well in control. Mary must have felt very isolated at Holyrood. In the lawless Borders of Scotland, the nobles were as likely to support the English as the Scottish Queen. They had rallied behind the Scottish crown at the battles of

"Welcome, illustrat lady and our queen:
welcome, our lion with the fleur-de-lis:
welcome, our thistle with the Lorraine green:
welcome, our rubent rose upon the ryce:
welcome, our gem and joyful genetrice:
welcome, our beill of Albion to beir:
welcome, our pleasant princess maist of price:
God give thee grace aganis this guid New Year!" *Alexander Scott, A New Year Gift to the Queen Mary when she come first hame, 1562.*

Opposite The artist W Hole's glorified version of Mary's entry into Edinburgh in 1561, in which the mist has happily lifted and the horses have revived.

Above Lord James Stewart, Earl of Moray, Mary's half-brother and adviser.

"**Her Majesty ordains ... that none ... take upon hand, privately or openly to make any alteration or innovation in the state of religion, or attempt anything against the same, which her Majesty found publicly and universally standing at her Majesty's arrival in this Realm, under pain of death.**" *Proclamation of 24th August, 1561 authorized by Mary.*

Flodden, Solway Moss and Pinkie Cleugh, only to bring suffering on themselves, so they were more interested in protecting their own territory than in supporting their Queen.

The third section of Scotland was the Highland area north of Stirling. Rough mountainous land set the Highlanders apart from the Lowlanders. The Highland clan system meant that people owed more to a family chief than to a distant monarch. In many parts of the Highlands only Gaelic was spoken, a language that sounded barbarous to Lowlander and Englishman alike. However, the Highlanders were still Catholics, and in George Gordon, Earl of Huntly, they had a leader who would have done anything asked of him by Mary.

Because of her ignorance of Scotland, Mary relied on her half-brother James Stewart for guidance. So on 24th August, 1561 Mary issued a proclamation at Edinburgh's Mercat Cross acknowledging the Protestant faith as the religion of Scotland. On 6th September she chose eight Protestants and only four Catholics to form her Privy Council. Maitland became Secretary of State and the Earl of Morton was made Chancellor. Now Lord James convinced Mary that it would be in her best interests to crush the power of Huntly, Scotland's foremost Catholic noble.

Huntly's son Sir John Gordon had escaped arrest for brawling in Edinburgh, and fled to the Gordon country, the north-east of Scotland. Lord James saw this as a chance to end Huntly's career and to gain for himself Huntly's lands in Moray. In August 1562, Mary and her half-brother rode north to Inverness, where they seized the castle. Then they returned to Aberdeen to defeat Huntly at Corrichie. Huntly himself died of a stroke, while Sir John Gordon was clumsily beheaded in front of Mary, who was ill at the sight of the execution. Lord James was already directing Mary towards policies that would benefit himself. He became Earl of Moray, but Mary had destroyed the one man in Scotland who could have raised a Catholic army for her.

By proclaiming toleration of the Protestant religion, by choosing Protestants to advise her, by destroying Huntly, Mary must have felt she had done enough to convince her subjects of her fairness in matters of religion. But whatever she did, her French ways made Protestants suspicious. They were sure she was working for the return of the Catholic Church, and could not forgive her for something she did on her first Sunday back in Scotland. What Mary did was to hold a private Mass in her private chapel at Holyrood. Her half-brother Moray assured her this would be acceptable, but in the event there was a riot and he personally safeguarded her by standing at the chapel door.

One man in particular was not willing to let the matter rest, even when the Queen's Mercat Cross proclamation of tolerance was made the next day. John Knox got up in his pulpit at St Giles to tell people that one Mass was more fearful than ten thousand armed enemies. "When we join hands with idolatry," preached Knox, "there is no doubt that both God's amicable presence and comfortable defence leave us." In France queens were not denounced like this. Mary thought that she would personally teach this humble preacher that he could not criticize the rightful Queen of Scots in her own realm.

> **"You are ower sair** [too deep] **for me."** *Mary Queen of Scots to Knox at their first interview, August 1561.*

Below John Knox in his pulpit, preaching to the Lords of the Congregation, as the Protestant Scottish nobles called themselves. Knox was known for his wit as well as his denunciations.

5 Knox and Mary

NO TWO CHARACTERS in Scottish history have been less alike than John Knox and Mary Stuart. In 1561, Mary was a tall, graceful, hazel-eyed, auburn-haired widow of nineteen, while Knox was a small, fierce, blue-eyed, black-bearded widower of fifty-six. Mary, daughter of a king, had spent most of her life in the sumptuous French court. Knox, son of a peasant, had spent part of his life in the French galleys. Mary was a devoted Catholic. Knox was a fanatical Protestant. In their five dramatic meetings it became certain that Scotland was not big enough for both of them.

Knox was first summoned to Holyrood for denouncing the Queen's private Mass. On 31st August, 1561 Mary accused him of inciting her subjects against their rightful Queen. Against this, Knox argued that God alone ruled over men and denied that monarchs had a divine right over their subjects. When Mary asked him whether he seriously believed that subjects had the right to oppose their rulers, Knox replied bluntly that if "princes exceed their bounds, Madam, no doubt they should be resisted even by power". It took a stunned Mary about twenty minutes to recover from this blatant remark. When she finally spoke, it was only to promise to "defend the Kirk of Rome, for I think it is the true Kirk of God".

December 1562 brought stories to Scotland of Guise persecution of the Huguenots. Hearing that Mary had danced until well after midnight, Knox was sure

Opposite John Knox reproving Mary. In their meetings, the Protestant preacher spoke bluntly to the Scottish Queen, sometimes reducing her to tears.

Overleaf Lochleven Castle, scene of one of Mary's least stormy meetings with John Knox in 1563. Later, the island castle was Mary's jail.

she was celebrating the persecution by her uncles. After a sermon on the vanity of princes, he was again summoned to Holyrood. He admitted that he disapproved of "fiddling and flinging" if it mocked God's law. Furthermore, he said that Mary's uncles were "enemies to God, and unto his son Jesus Christ". This was a deliberate insult, and Mary dismissed him. Knox calmly said that as he had often faced angry men, he could not possibly be afraid of "the pleasing face of a Gentlewoman".

By now Mary realized that in Knox she faced a serious challenge to her authority, a man who had no respect for rank. Very well, she would try to charm him. In April 1563 she was staying on the island of Lochleven with Moray's mother Lady Margaret Erskine Douglas. She sent for Knox so they might discuss religious toleration before supper. Next morning, when she was hawking at Kinross, she spoke to him again and appealed for his help in healing the religious wounds of the nation. Knox was courteous and almost pleasant. They parted on good terms.

It was a truce that lasted only two months, for when Knox heard that Mary was once more considering a marriage with Don Carlos of Catholic Spain, he went to St Giles to denounce the marriage because "all Papists are infidels." Mary was in a rage when she summoned Knox to Holyrood. "What", she demanded, "have you to do with my marriage? Or what are you within this commonwealth?" Knox's now celebrated reply completely floored Mary. "A subject born within the same, madam," he answered the Queen. Mary was reduced to a flood of tears. She, a queen, had been publicly humiliated by the son of a peasant.

At the end of the year Mary saw a chance to get rid of Knox. A private Mass at Holyrood had been interrupted by the Protestants. When Knox supported those arrested for the offence, Mary had him up before her Privy Council on a charge of high treason. She even gloated openly at the prospect of his downfall. Knox had made *her* weep, she laughed, so now she would make *him* weep. But there were no tears from the preacher. Nor was Mary's Privy Council likely to go against the symbol of their faith. As usual, Knox talked his way out of the charge against him and was acquitted. Mary was once again humiliated.

Knox was simply too powerful, too much in control of the situation for Mary. Everything he did was presented as the work of God. On 26th March 1564 the 59-year-old preacher married 17-year-old Margaret Stewart, but no one dared criticize Knox to his face. Mary must have envied him his ability to do as he liked, for she too was thinking of marriage. For her it was not a simple choice: too many other people were involved in making a match.

Knox had created an atmosphere in which it would be difficult for Mary to marry a Catholic. Now Elizabeth I had her say. She suggested that Mary should marry her own favourite, Lord Robert Dudley, although he was not of royal blood. Mary took this suggestion as a personal insult, but it was more likely that the English Queen only wanted a loyal subject at the Scottish court to guard against the threat of Spanish or French influence. At the end of 1564 Mary rejected Elizabeth's proposal.

Insanity ruled out two other possibilities. As the result of a fall Don Carlos was mentally unfit for anything, while Châtelherault's son Young Arran had become demented. There was one other possibility, the exiled Earl of Lennox's English-born son Lord Darnley (1546–67), whom Mary had met and found attractive. As a grandson of Margaret Tudor, Darnley was Mary's cousin and after her in line to the English throne. This put Elizabeth I against the match, and the Protestant nobles opposed it because Darnley was a Catholic. But instead of heeding this advice and acting like a queen, Mary acted like a human being in love.

Below Lord Robert Dudley, Earl of Leicester. He was Elizabeth I's choice for a husband for Mary.

6 The Second Marriage

MARY CERTAINLY FOUND Henry Stuart, Lord Darnley, attractive—in fact "the properest and best proportioned long man" she had ever seen. Otherwise, why would the Queen of Scots have been willing to act as nurse to her cousin when, in April 1565, he lay ill with measles at Stirling Castle? She wanted him for her husband and it was enough for her that she had the approval of Philip II and Charles IX, the new French King. However, Mary did not live in France or Spain. By now she knew how much Elizabeth I opposed her marriage to Darnley, while in Scotland itself the Protestants did not want to have a Catholic king as well as a Catholic queen. Moray warned Mary that she would have to go to Parliament for advice.

Up to this point, Mary had relied on the judgment of her half-brother. True, he had made himself the strongest man in Scotland through her, but he had also protected her and guided her wisely on religious policy. Now she decided she could do without Moray. She ignored the authority of Parliament and proclaimed her cousin King Henry of Scotland. Then on 29th July, 1565 she married Darnley in a Catholic ceremony in Holyrood. Moray was bitter enough to rebel against the marriage.

Mary had gained an attractive husband and lost a powerful half-brother. On 6th August, Moray was outlawed, and later that month Mary and Darnley rode out of Edinburgh with their troops to put down his rebellion. While they were out of Edinburgh, Moray rode back into the capital, but he had to leave again for lack

"None of this was apparent to Mary Queen of Scots at her first meeting with her cousin [Darnley] in Scotland, at Wemyss Castle. She merely saw and admired his charming exterior, which, like a delightful red shiny apple ready for the eating, gave no hint of the maggots which lay inside."
Antonia Fraser, Mary Queen of Scots, 1969.

Opposite Mary and Lord Darnley, from a mezzotint by Dunkerton. It was based on the portrait by the Belgian-born Renold Elstracke, one of the earliest engravers in England.

33

of support. This so-called Chaseabout Rebellion ended when Elizabeth I granted Moray not the English troops he wanted, but only an offer of asylum in England. On 6th October, Moray fled across the Scottish Border and the rebellion was over. His position as Mary's strong man was taken by James Hepburn, Earl of Bothwell, Hereditary Admiral of Scotland (1536–78), who was now created Lieutenant-General of the East, Middle and West Marches.

With the defeat of Moray, Mary looked forward to a period of peace with her husband. Instead, Darnley spoiled all chances of tranquillity. He became more arrogant, demanding and insulting with every day that passed. He wanted the Crown Matrimonial, he wanted more money, he wanted to spend his days hunting and his nights drinking. Where there had been charm, there was now petulance; where respect, abuse. Besides, Mary had a new interest. By the time she went to Linlithgow Palace in December 1565, the whole court knew she was pregnant. Possessing the mentality of a spoiled child, Darnley was not ready for a rival, even if that rival was his own child. He felt himself destined to be the subject of his own son, should that child be male.

But what if it were not his child? Moray and the other exiled Chaseabout Rebels knew that, unless something drastic was done, they would lose all their properties at the Parliament due to meet on 12th March, 1566. They had had a poor reception in England, where Elizabeth I made it clear that she disapproved of armed resistance. They returned to Scotland, where the one weapon they could depend on was the insane jealousy of Darnley. If he could be persuaded that his wife was pregnant by another man, then he could be made to do anything. Moray had already proved effective at influencing Mary. It would be easier still to guide the foolish Darnley. And if regaining his power meant replacing Mary by Darnley, then so be it.

All the Protestant nobles needed for such a plan was an idiotic king, a well-placed trouble maker, and a rival. In Darnley they had their perfect fool, and in the Earl of Morton a natural schemer. All they had to do was to invent a lover for Mary.

David Riccio (1533–66), a 33-year-old Italian, had come to the Scottish court in 1561 as companion to the ambassador of Savoy. He was not at all physically attractive, but his cultured conversation, elegant dress and musical ability appealed to Mary. In 1564 she appointed Riccio her French Secretary and continued to enjoy his company. This was not so surprising, as her husband had his own ways of passing time. When Darnley was with the Queen he was likely to have her in tears, so she turned to Riccio. As a foreigner, he was resented by the Scotsmen in Mary's court, and as a Catholic he aroused the hatred of the nobles, who were sure he was a Papal spy. It was Morton's task to convince Darnley that David Riccio was not only Mary's friend, but also her lover, even the father of the child she was bearing. Darnley did not need much persuasion.

At the beginning of March 1566, the conspirators decided it was time to involve Darnley in their plan. They had to strike before the Parliament of 12th March, so they had a bond ready. Moray and Morton signed the document and insisted that Darnley put his own name to it. On the surface, the bond committed them to three things. First, that Darnley should be given the Crown Matrimonial (which meant that in the event of Mary's death, he would succeed as King in his own right). Second, that the Chaseabout Rebels should be returned to Scotland and given their properties. Third, that the Protestant religion should be safeguarded. Murder was not mentioned in the bond, but in the minds of the conspirators there was a way of killing three birds with one stone. If the pregnant Queen were given a terrible shock who could say she would not die of it?

Above Mary and Darnley's ring, dated 1565—the year of their marriage.

7 Murder of Riccio

ON SATURDAY EVENING 9th March, 1566 Mary Queen of Scots entertained five guests in the tiny supper room that lay next to her bedroom. As a woman six months pregnant she felt somewhat fragile and much in need of peace and quiet. She had decided to relax in an intimate company that included her secretary David Riccio. It was to be a pleasant evening of conversation and cards and perhaps a little music. Meat was to be served for supper. Certainly the last person the little group expected to see was Darnley. Although his apartments lay below those of the Queen, with a privy staircase connecting the two royal bedrooms, Darnley by now preferred the night life of Edinburgh to the company of his wife.

When Darnley suddenly emerged from the privy staircase and entered the supper room the Queen was surprised, but if he had come to share supper with her, then Mary was pleased to see him. The next event astonished her. Lord Ruthven, a notoriously wicked noble who was thought to be lying on his death-bed, now appeared unannounced in his Queen's private supper room. Even more astonishing, he was armed and rudely demanded of the Queen that "yonder man David come forth of your privy chamber where he hath been overlong".

When the Queen in turn demanded an explanation of his conduct, Ruthven dared to lecture her. She was wrong, he said, to be familiar with Riccio and wrong to outlaw the Chaseabout Rebels. As Ruthven put his hand on his dagger the terrified little Italian rushed to

> **"Parole, parole, nothing but words. The Scots will boast but rarely perform their brags."**
> *David Riccio.*

Opposite The murder of David Riccio in Mary's bedroom at Holyrood, 1566, by Lord Ruthven and his followers.

hold the Queen's skirts. There was little she could do but protest as six Ruthven followers charged into the room armed with pistols and daggers. They grabbed Riccio and pulled him roughly from the Queen. *"Sauvez ma vie, madame,"* Riccio cried as they dragged him across the floor of Mary's bedroom, *"Sauvez ma vie."* No one could possibly have saved his life. At the door connecting the royal bedroom with Mary's audience chamber David Riccio was stabbed more than fifty times.

Mary had never lacked courage and now she shocked Darnley into a shamed silence by the violent expression of her anger. Ruthven, however, refused to be silenced by the Queen. He swaggered back into the supper room, called for wine, and again lectured Mary on her friendship with Riccio. He knew that Mary was in no position to carry out any threats she might make. Morton and his Douglas clansmen had taken control of Holyrood Palace. Bothwell (who had been in the palace but not in the supper room itself) escaped out of a back window. Mary was quite alone, at the mercy of the men who had just murdered Riccio. Already one of Ruthven's henchmen had pointed a pistol at her stomach. Now another threatened to cut her into pieces if she dared to go to the window to cry for help.

It is certain that one of the murderers' aims had been to frighten Mary into miscarrying her child. Otherwise why did they seize Riccio in her presence and threaten her own life? Riccio was only a servant. If he had been the main target, he could have been murdered quietly without having the Queen as a witness. In the sixteenth century a miscarriage often meant death for the mother as well as the child. While Mary knew that the conspirators would hardly dare assassinate her, she also knew that they would welcome her death from what they could claim to be natural causes. Mary had to reach safety with her unborn child, and to do this she was even willing to use Darnley.

On the Sunday morning Mary was ready for her husband. She was pleasant to him, and easily convinced him that he had no real future with the Protestant lords

Opposite Mary inspired poets and artists from her day to ours. This portrait seems to show her saddened by her misfortunes but still young and beautiful.

who had murdered Riccio. After all, these were the same men who had rebelled against the Queen when she had chosen him for her husband. She told Darnley the nobles were only using him until it was safe for them to get rid of him. By Monday she was ready for the murderers. She pretended that she intended to pardon them, and when Moray arrived she greeted him as a long-lost brother, not as a man who had been willing to raise an army against her. It was an impressive performance. None suspected that she would escape that night.

At midnight Mary and Darnley left Holyrood by the servants' quarters. They had to ride 30 km (20 miles) to the safety of Dunbar Castle. For a pregnant woman such a journey was a terrible ordeal, and she complained to Darnley. "If this baby dies", he told her, "we can have more." This convinced her of his lack of feelings towards their child. They made their journey in five hours—five hours of agony and worry for Mary.

On reaching Dunbar, Mary acted with great speed as she was determined to overcome this latest threat to her throne. The Earl of Bothwell helped her to raise an army of eight thousand men within days. On 17th March the Queen led this army into Edinburgh—to the horror of Morton and Ruthven, who fled over the Border. Moray had been out of Edinburgh on the night of the Riccio murder, and Mary was willing to give him a pardon because his support was essential. Darnley, on the other hand, could not be forgiven. He had endangered her life and the life of her child. He could not be allowed to do so again.

Opposite "The Flight of Mary Queen of Scots", an engraving after Westall by Francesco Bartolozzi, a Florentine who settled in London in 1764. One of the original members of the Royal Academy, he engraved its diploma, which is still in use.

8 Murder of Darnley

ON 19TH JUNE, 1566 Mary gave birth to a son, James (1566–1625), in Edinburgh Castle. The city celebrated in a riot of bonfires. Not only was the Stuart succession assured in Scotland, there was every likelihood that Mary's son would become King of England too. The unmarried Elizabeth I acknowledged as much when she lamented: "Alack, the Queen of Scots is lighter of a bonny son, and I am but of barren stock." Darnley was brought before the child and told by Mary: "My Lord, God has given you and me a son, begotten by none but you." And in case he missed the point she added: "This is your son and no other man's son. I am desirous that all here, with ladies and others bear witness." She had not forgotten the accusations about Riccio.

Although the stress of that murder and the strain of a difficult birth had badly affected Mary's health, Darnley chose this moment to talk of leaving his wife and quitting Scotland. Mary, he claimed, did not honour him enough, and the Protestant lords had no respect for him. This was of course true. Moray was back in favour and had no need of Darnley. As for the Earl of Bothwell, he had been lucky to escape with his life on the night of the Riccio murder, and was not a man to overlook insults. Bothwell had helped Mary at the time of the Chaseabout Rebellion, and had come to her side when she escaped to Dunbar. Now, according to Elizabeth I's ambassador, Sir Henry Killigrew, Bothwell's "credit with the Queen is more than all the rest together".

On 7th October, 1566, Bothwell was badly wounded in a Border skirmish with the Elliots and retired to Her-

> **"Pity me, kinsmen, for the sake of Jesus Christ, who pitied all the world."** *Lord Darnley, in his last plea to his murderers.*

Opposite Mary dancing with the Earl of Bothwell at the wedding masque of her French valet, just before Darnley's death. Did either know what was going to happen?

43

Above The Palace of Holyrood, where Mary spent most of her time in Scotland. It was here that Riccio was murdered in her bedroom, and here she spent the night of Darnley's murder.

mitage Castle in Liddesdale to recover. Mary had gone on legal business to Jedburgh, but when she heard of Bothwell's condition, she and Moray rode over to see him and returned the same day. After this 80 km (50-mile) journey, Mary's health collapsed. She suffered from nervous strain, as well as physical exhaustion. For a while she lost her speech and seemed on the point of death. Darnley briefly interrupted his hawking and hunting to visit his wife in Jedburgh, but if he was concerned for the woman who was once his nurse, he did not show it. He left her the next day.

By November Mary had recovered sufficiently to move to Craigmillar Castle near Edinburgh. She was so depressed she said openly: "I could wish to be dead." She was in fact sick to death of Darnley, and so were the men who came to see her at Craigmillar. Moray and Maitland were as ambitious as ever. The Earl of Argyll suspected Darnley of Popish plotting, and Bothwell already had an eye on Darnley's throne. Mary discussed divorce with the nobles, but rejected it because it might affect her son's chances of succeeding her. Maitland asked her to let the nobles find a solution to her problems. They would "find the means", he said, in return for a pardon for Morton. Mary agreed but did not press for details.

On 17th December Mary's son received his Catholic baptism in great ceremony at Stirling Castle. Elizabeth I sent a gold font, while Moray, Bothwell and Argyll dressed in their splendid best for the event. Darnley was conspicuous by his absence. At the end of the month he left for Glasgow, where he fell ill with smallpox. There were rumours that he planned to overthrow his

Left William Maitland, Mary's Secretary of State. An ambitious Protestant, he may have conspired in the murders of Riccio and Darnley.

wife so that he himself could rule Scotland as the champion of Catholicism. Perhaps to keep an eye on her deceitful husband, Mary had him brought back to Edinburgh in January 1567. He refused to convalesce at Craigmillar Castle, but instead he moved into the old provost's house at Kirk o'Field, just outside Edinburgh's town wall. With a taffeta mask hiding his disfigured face Darnley was lodged in an upstairs bedroom, above a room provided for the use of the Queen.

Mary planned to stay at Kirk o'Field on Sunday, 9th February. It was the last Sabbath before Lent, a day of celebration for a Catholic. So that her husband would not feel cut off from the merrymaking, Mary, in the company of Bothwell and others, rode to Kirk o'Field in the evening. They talked and played dice until about 11 p.m., when Mary told Darnley that she could not stay the night because she had promised to attend the wedding masque of her French valet Bastian Pages. Mary and Bothwell then left Kirk o'Field to return to Holyrood.

At 2 a.m. on the Monday a great explosion blew up the old provost's house. Had he still been in the house, Darnley would have been killed, but he had used a rope and dropped 5 m (14 ft) from his room so that he could get away. He got only as far as the hands of a strangler, and was found in his night-shirt without the trace of a burn.

Exactly what happened no one will ever know for sure. Either Darnley had hatched a gunpowder plot to destroy Mary, who had been expected to spend the night in the house, then, when the plan misfired, he was murdered by one of his many enemies. Or Bothwell may have planned the whole thing to get rid of Darnley. Bothwell may have had the house blown up and his Hepburn kinsmen standing by in case Darnley escaped. When he did, they strangled him. If Bothwell was the culprit, then it is likely that Moray, Maitland and Morton were in on the plan. We can be almost certain that Mary knew nothing about it yet it was she who had to suffer the consequences.

Opposite This engraving is called "Death of Lord Darnley" but, as he was found strangled in his nightshirt out of doors, it is a decidedly romantic picture!

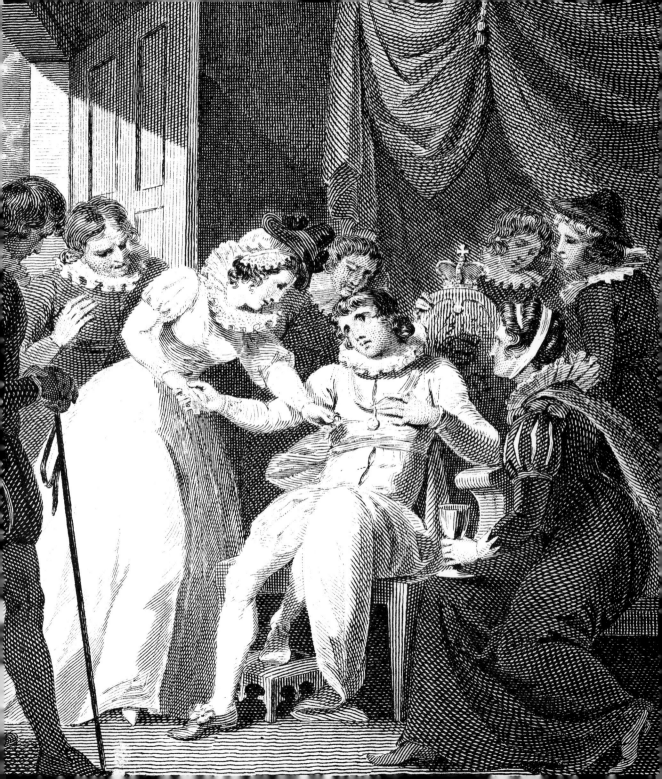

9 The Third Marriage

MORE SURPRISED than saddened by her husband's death, Mary spent a week in official mourning then sought the fresh air of Seton to clear her mind. The air of Edinburgh was foul with suspicion and gossip. Everyone was sure that Bothwell was the murderer, and there were even placards accusing Mary of a part in the Kirk o'Field affair. A reward of £2,000 for information leading to the arrest of the murderer was never claimed—too many of Scotland's nobles were involved in the plots to get rid of Darnley. Moray conveniently removed himself to London, while Maitland wanted the murder to pass into history. Bothwell, the chief suspect, had ambitious plans of his own.

Only Darnley's outraged father, the Earl of Lennox, was prepared to do something about the murder. He had no intention of letting Bothwell get away with it. Under pressure from Lennox, Mary had no alternative but to agree to a parliamentary enquiry into the matter. Bothwell duly appeared, accompanied by Morton and Maitland and his armed Hepburn kinsmen, but Lennox did not show up. He knew that the six companions allowed him by law were no match for Bothwell and his henchmen. As no case was laid against him, Bothwell was duly acquitted by Parliament.

Bothwell's next step was to make himself King. He had given Mary loyal service in her hour of need, and used her gratitude to make himself the most powerful noble in Scotland. The Queen knew that Bothwell was a strong man and a useful ally, small and battle worn though he was. Now she was to have further proof of his masterful nature. Protected by two hundred Hepburn kinsmen, Bothwell entertained twenty-eight

> **"The judgment of the people is that the Queen will marry Bothwell."** *Sir William Drury to William Cecil, 29th March, 1567.*

Opposite Carberry Hill, outside Edinburgh, where Mary agreed to give herself up to the confederate army.

lords, including Morton and Maitland, at Ainslie's Tavern in Edinburgh on 19th April. Assuring his guests that the Queen approved of what he was doing, he persuaded them to sign a bond agreeing to his marriage to Mary. It certainly convinced her that Bothwell had the support of the Protestant nobles, which she knew was essential to her own survival, but it did not convince her that marriage was the answer. Not yet, anyway.

Bothwell was not prepared to wait for her decision. As the Queen returned after visiting her son at Stirling, she was suddenly approached by Bothwell and the Hepburns at the Bridges of Almond, 10 km (6 miles) from Edinburgh. Mary had Maitland with her, plus thirty horsemen. Bothwell had eight hundred men. He told Mary that her life would be in danger if she returned to Edinburgh and she must go with him to Dunbar Castle for her own safety. Rather than cause bloodshed, Mary told her men that she was willing to go with Bothwell. As far as Bothwell was concerned, the Queen was now his to have and to hold. Bothwell already had a wife, Lady Jean Gordon, but he soon arranged a divorce.

On 15th May, three months after the murder of Darnley, Mary married Bothwell in a Protestant ceremony at Holyrood. Once again, she was risking everything on the strength of her husband's character. But she had loved Darnley, and she did not love Bothwell. In fact he made her very unhappy. Philip du Croc, the French ambassador, wrote to Catherine de Medici saying that two days after her wedding "being secluded all day with the Earl of Bothwell, she cried out aloud for someone to give her a knife so she could kill herself".

There were other differences too. Mary had married Darnley against the advice of Elizabeth I and Moray. In marrying Bothwell, she felt there was no one else to turn to. Elizabeth always gave refuge to those who rebelled against Mary, while Moray had been involved in plots to depose her. Bothwell seemed to be the only Scotsman strong enough to keep her on her throne.

The most serious difference of all was that Darnley

had been a fool, but Bothwell was the man widely believed to be the murderer of her previous husband. Mary was quite mistaken in thinking that the Protestant nobles supported her marriage to Bothwell. Ainslie's Tavern bond was not worth the paper it was written on, and the Protestant lords promptly raised a confederate army against Mary and Bothwell. The marriage not only had Scotland up in arms—all Europe was shocked.

Bothwell and Mary fled to the south after they were refused entrance to Edinburgh Castle, pursued by the confederate army. On 15th June at Carberry Hill, 13 km (8 miles) east of Edinburgh, the two sides finally met. Du Croc, speaking on behalf of the nobles, asked Mary to hand Bothwell over. She agreed to give herself up on two conditions: that she would be treated as Queen of Scots, and that Bothwell would get a safe conduct to Dunbar.

Bothwell got away all right—to a Danish prison, where he died insane. But Mary was betrayed by the nobles. She was taken by jeering soldiers to a house in Edinburgh, in which she spent a sleepless night. Next day she appeared at the window—her hair dishevelled, her breasts naked—crying out for help. In the evening she was taken 80 km (50 miles) to Lochleven Castle, where she had once debated with John Knox.

10 Abdication and Flight

AS SOON AS she arrived at Lochleven Castle on 17th June, 1567, Mary collapsed into a coma that lasted for two weeks. She had stayed at the island castle in 1562 as the guest of Moray's mother Lady Margaret Erskine Douglas and his half-brother Sir William Douglas. Now she was their prisoner. Bothwell had failed in a last attempt to raise support for Mary and had been formally outlawed on 17th July. About the same time, Mary, who was about three months pregnant, miscarried Bothwell's twins.

While she was still recovering, Mary was forced to abdicate in favour of her son. She knew that if she ever escaped, the abdication would not be considered legal, while if she did not give up her throne it would be an easy matter for the nobles to get rid of her. On 29th July, her thirteen-month-old son was crowned James VI in a Protestant church outside Stirling Castle, and her half-brother Moray was proclaimed Regent. In December, the Privy Council learned of documents said to implicate Mary in the murder of Darnley, which gave Moray enough evidence to have Mary imprisoned.

Fortunately for Mary she still had her legendary charm. Sir William Douglas's brother George and cousin Willy worshipped her, and planned to free the captive Queen. In the spring of 1568, George Douglas picked a quarrel with his brother so that he could leave the island to arrange an escape from the loch shore. Willy was left to play his part on the island. On 2nd May, he involved the Queen in a seemingly harmless pageant, during which he stole the castle keys from Sir

> **"When prevailed upon to sign her abdication, she was lying on her bed in a state of very great weakness, partly in consequence of a great flux, the result of a miscarriage of twins, her issue by Bothwell."** *Claude Nau, Memorials of Mary Stuart, 1883.*

Opposite Mary's son James. He was James VI of Scotland from 1567 and James I of England from 1603 until his death in 1625. He relied on his courtiers and was called "the wisest fool in Christendom".

Above Mary forced to sign her
abdication at Lochleven Castle in
1567.

William Douglas. Then Willy rowed Mary, disguised
as a countrywoman, to the shore where George was
waiting with horses. Mary's ten months of island captivity were at an end. Now she was anxious to get her
own back on Moray.

It did not take Mary long to raise five thousand men,
but still Moray refused to negotiate with her, leaving
her no alternative but to test her strength in battle. With
more men than Moray, she should have won when they
met at Langside on 13th May. However, Moray had
the warlike Morton to command his troops, while Mary

had to rely on the inexperienced Earl of Argyll. Mary's army was humiliated, and the Queen of Scots fled to the Catholic south-west of Scotland. Some of her followers urged her to gather a new army. Others said she should flee to the safety of France. Mary made up her own mind. She would throw herself on the mercy of her cousin Elizabeth I. Although she had never met the Queen and had never ratified the Treaty of Edinburgh recognizing Elizabeth I as Queen of England, Mary crossed the Solway on 16th May. She would never see Scotland again.

Above Mary leaves Scotland after her defeat at Langside, hoping for help from Elizabeth I.

She arrived in England with sixteen followers, no horses, and no money. All she had was faith in God and Elizabeth I. It was not, alas, enough. Mary was conducted first to Carlisle Castle then to Bolton Castle in Yorkshire. She could not understand why she was not being taken to see her cousin Elizabeth I. When she was told that the English felt her problems could best be solved by an enquiry into the charges of murder being made against her by Moray, she was amazed. But, believing that Elizabeth I would restore her to the Scottish throne on finding her innocent, she agreed to co-operate.

Mary wrote frequently to Elizabeth requesting a personal interview. When the letters failed she wrote a sonnet to the English Queen which perfectly sums up her feelings on finding herself in England as "the sport of Fate":

"A longing haunts my spirit day and night
Bitter and sweet, torments my aching heart
Between doubt and fear, it holds its wayward part,
And while it lingers, rest and peace take flight.

Dear sister, if these lines too boldly speak
Of my fond wish to see you, 'tis for this—
That I repine and sink in bitterness,
If still denied the favour that I seek.

I have seen a ship freed from control
On the high seas, outside a friendly port,
And what was peaceful change to woe and pain;

Even so am I, a lonely, trembling soul,
Fearing—not you, but to be made the sport
Of Fate, that bursts the closest, strongest chain."

Mary could have saved her eloquence—her fate was already sealed. She was too much of a threat to the English crown and too much of a rival for Elizabeth I. What Mary had taken for a friendly port was to become her prison.

Opposite Mary, supposedly disguised as a countrywoman, escaping from Lochleven. The gallant William Douglas is helping her into a rowing boat.

11 The Silver Casket

AS MARY'S CAREER so clearly shows, the Scottish nobles would do anything to protect their own interests. They would change sides, conspire against their Queen, even murder if it suited them. Yet Mary was to be accused of planning the murder of Darnley by the very men who stood to gain most from that murder, the very men who had disliked Darnley from the start. She could expect anything from them but loyalty. Moray, Maitland and Morton were determined to remain in control of Scotland. As Mary was an obstacle in their way, they would have to get rid of her one way or another.

It was Morton who claimed to have come into possession of the so-called Casket Letters. On 19th June, 1567, according to his version of the facts, he was dining in Edinburgh with Maitland when he heard that three of Bothwell's servants had been captured. One of these servants had, under a bed in an Edinburgh house, "a certain silver box, overgilt, containing divers missive writings, sonnets, contracts and obligations for marriage between the Queen . . . and James sometime Earl of Bothwell". In other words, the casket contained eight personal letters, two marriage contracts and a love-ballad in twelve stanzas. By 15th December the Scottish Parliament could pardon the nobles for treason against the Queen because on the evidence of "her privy letters written wholly with her own hand . . . it is most certain that she was privy, art and part, of the actual devise and deed of the fore-named murder of the King, her lawful husband".

When Elizabeth's enquiry on the Darnley murder

Opposite The Earl of Morton, Mary's Chancellor and a probable plotter in the assassinations of Riccio and Darnley. He was Regent of Scotland in 1572 and ended on the scaffold.

> **"I never writ anything concerning that matter to any creature. There are divers in Scotland, both men and women, that can counterfeit my handwriting."** *Mary Queen of Scots, on the Casket Letters.*

Right Facsimile of Mary's signature. She always used the French form "Marie". Her writing looks easy enough for a forger to copy.

was held in York in October 1568, Moray showed the letters to the English Commissioners. Their reaction was to tell Elizabeth that "the said letters and ballads do discover such inordinate love between her and Bothwell, her loathing and abhorrence of her husband that was murdered, in such sort as every good and godly man cannot but detest and abhor the same." There was no doubt of Mary's guilt, they added, "if the said letters be written with her own hand". But were they?

Though the original documents conveniently disappeared from history there is little doubt that Mary was "framed" by the Scottish nobles. Four of the eight letters were written by her and none of these is in any way criminal. The other four letters and the love-ballad were written to Bothwell by another woman, probably

Above Bolton Castle, one of the many castle prisons in which Mary stayed, in relative comfort, during her nineteen years in England.

his Norwegian girlfriend Anna Throndsen, and naturally these letters declare a passionate love for Bothwell. By mixing the two sets of letters together, it was made to look as if Mary had been in love with Bothwell while Darnley was still alive. It was probably Maitland who tampered with the letters to make it seem as if Mary had a motive for planning Darnley's murder. He could easily have had Anna's letters forged in Mary's hand because he had married one of the four Maries, Mary Fleming, who had been taught by the same writing master as the Queen of Scots.

The English Commission, headed by the Duke of Norfolk, moved from York to Westminster and finally to Hampton Court. On 26th November, 1568 Moray was allowed to present his accusation of Mary as the murderer of Darnley. Three days later Darnley's outraged father, the Earl of Lennox, insisted that Mary had been involved in the murder of her husband, his son. On 7th December the casket itself, "a small gilded coffer of not fully one foot long", was produced.

Although the Commission had seen Moray, Lennox and the infamous casket, Mary was not allowed to appear before them. When she wrote to the Commission saying that the nobles were guilty of the murder, her accusation was ignored. Instead, Elizabeth suggested to Mary that she should abdicate again. But throughout her life Mary had always refused to ratify the Treaty of Edinburgh recognizing Elizabeth I as rightful Queen of England, and equally she always refused to abdicate, apart from the time she was made to give up the crown at Lochleven.

By now, the English Government had decided what to do. Moray was given a £5,000 loan and given leave to return to Scotland as Regent. Then the Commission gave their inconclusive verdict that "There had been nothing sufficiently produced nor shown by [the Protestant nobles] against the Queen their Sovereign, whereby the Queen of England should conceive or take any evil opinion of the Queen, her good sister, for anything yet seen." Despite this statement, Mary was to serve what amounted to life imprisonment, for she was never allowed to leave England. Elizabeth I had Mary under supervision, and the Regent Moray had control of Scotland. Her chief enemies were satisfied.

But Mary had no intention of becoming old as a captive queen. She knew there was a chance that Spain or France or the Pope would come to her assistance, and if not she had supporters in England itself. Already the Duke of Norfolk, although he had not met Mary, was thinking of marrying her. This in itself should have shown how little the Casket Letters proved, because it is hardly likely that the premier duke of England would consider marrying a woman he really believed to be capable of murdering her husband. There was still hope for Mary.

Opposite A portrait of Mary in 1578, when she was thirty-six. In her later years she suffered badly from rheumatism and dropsy.

MARIA
G
SCOTIA
SIMA·REGINA
ANCIÆ·DOTARIA
ANNO
ÆTATISREGNIQ
36·
ANCLICÆ·CAPTIVIT
19
S   H
1578

Lo Burleigh

Sr Fr Walfingham.

12 Elizabeth and Mary

ALTHOUGH MARY SPENT the last nineteen years of her life as a prisoner of her cousin Elizabeth I, she was never allowed to meet the English Queen. When Mary crossed over into England she gambled on Elizabeth's help, but it was a gamble that could not succeed because Elizabeth was not a woman to take chances. Mary had become a queen in the first week of her life. She was brought up in the luxury of the French court as the future Queen of France, fussed over, idolized by poets, and treated as a divine being, a Roman Catholic in a Roman Catholic country. Elizabeth had no such luck at the beginning of her life.

Henry VIII had invited the scorn of Catholic Europe when he divorced Catherine of Aragon to marry Anne Boleyn. When Anne could produce only a daughter, Elizabeth, instead of the male heir he wanted, Henry had his second wife beheaded and Elizabeth declared illegitimate. Thus from the beginning Elizabeth was un-acceptable to Catholics and even rejected by her own father. She was restored to her place in the succession after Henry got his male heir from his third wife Jane Seymour. But at most, all Elizabeth could hope to be was half-sister of an English king.

When Edward VI died from consumption at the age of fourteen, his place was taken by Catherine of Aragon's daughter Mary Tudor. A fanatical Catholic, Mary married Philip II of Spain and together they began a period of religious persecution which saw three hundred Protestants die at the stake in four years. In such a situation Elizabeth, the symbol of Protestant

Above Henry VIII (1491–1547), father of Mary I and Elizabeth I.

Opposite Elizabeth I with her advisers William Cecil and Sir Francis Walsingham.

hopes, became implicated in a plot in 1554 against "Bloody Mary" Tudor. She was sent to the Tower of London, narrowly escaping execution.

On the death of "Bloody Mary", Elizabeth succeeded to the throne as a woman of twenty-one experienced in hardship. She knew that monarchs were not divine but had to earn the respect of their subjects. She knew, too, that in France the young Queen of Scots was claiming the English crown. Elizabeth I was thus hardened to the reality of power while Mary remained sheltered in the world of the French court. All through her life Mary was unable to understand large issues. She was puzzled by Elizabeth's anger over her claim to the English throne. She took the death of Francis II as a personal tragedy, whereas it involved much of Europe. She was unaware that Catherine de Medici disliked her for reasons of power not personality.

Elizabeth developed a middle way in religion, but Mary became the Catholic monarch of a newly Protestant country. Although no fanatic in her religion, Mary's whole attitude was French, a fact that offended her Scottish subjects. Elizabeth was too shrewd to make a foolish mess of her private life, but Mary let her heart rule her head. She married Darnley against the advice of Elizabeth I and the Scottish Protestant nobles, and she married Bothwell when such a marriage was bound to shock the whole of Europe. Elizabeth I remained unmarried and kept her head.

However, Mary cannot be blamed for the treachery of the Scottish nobles. Elizabeth was able to rely on the sound advice of William Cecil for forty years, but Mary had no one man she could trust. Moray rebelled against her, and her Secretary Maitland, one of the ablest men of his time, earned the nickname "the Chameleon" for changing sides. In England the Tudors had established a strong monarchy, but in Scotland the crown had taken a battering with James IV at Flodden in 1513 (when ten thousand Scots were slain) and again with James V at Solway Moss. Elizabeth was ruthless against enemies; Mary pardoned rebels time after time.

The best indication of Elizabeth's attitude to her captive cousin comes in a poem written by the English Queen:

"The dread of future foes exiles my present joy,
And wit me warns to shun such snares as threaten mine
    annoy.
For falsehood now doth flow, and subject's faith doth
    ebb;
Which would not be if Reason ruled, or Wisdom
    weaved the Web.
But clouds of toys untried do cloak aspiring minds,
Which turn to rain of late repent by course of
    changed winds.
The top of hope supposed the root of ruth will be,
And fruitless all their graffed guiles, as shortly ye shall
    see.
Those dazzled eyes with pride, which great ambition
    blinds,
Shall be unsealed by worthy wights whose foresight
    falsehood finds.
The Daughter of Debate, that eke discord doth sow,
Shall reap no gain where former rule hath taught still
    peace to grow.
No foreign banished wight shall anchor in this port;
Our realm it brooks no stranger's force, let them else-
    where resort.
Our rusty sword with rest shall first his edge employ,
To poll their tops that seek such change and gape for
    joy."

Mary, "the Daughter of Debate", was indeed to
sow discord for Elizabeth.

Above The Bell Tower in the Tower of London, where Elizabeth was imprisoned by her sister, while Mary Queen of Scots was enjoying the luxury of the French court.

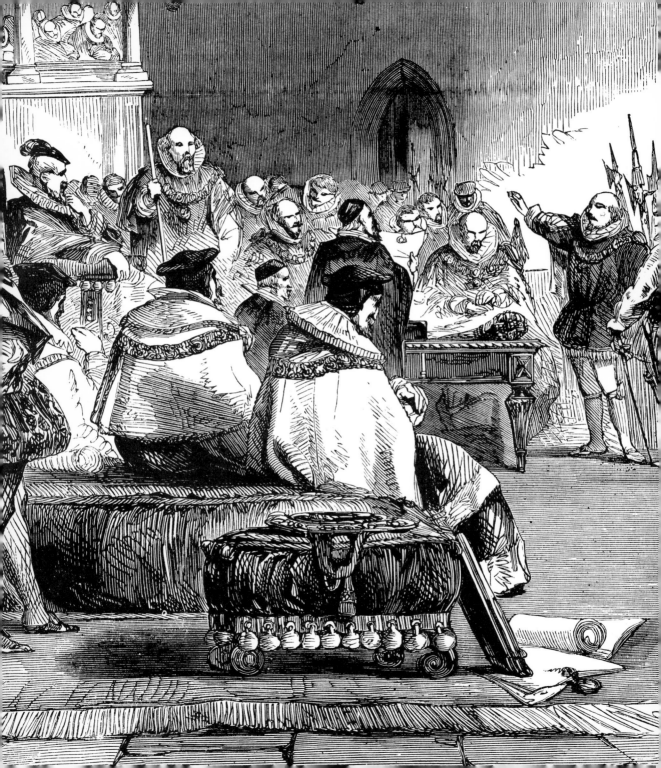

13 Life Imprisonment

FOR ANYONE BUT A QUEEN the conditions of Mary's life imprisonment would not seem bad by sixteenth-century standards. She had a court of about forty people, including her hairdresser Mary Seton and her valet Bastian Pages. For fourteen years she was under the custody of the Earl of Shrewsbury and stayed mainly in his property at Sheffield Castle and Sheffield Lodge. She spent much time embroidering and enjoyed occasional visits to the baths at Buxton. Two things, however, plagued these years: the physical agony of dropsy and rheumatic gout, and the pain of being shut away from public life.

It was her determination to return to public life that involved her in various plots. The first of these was formed by the Duke of Norfolk, who had headed the English enquiry into the Darnley murder. In 1569 Norfolk planned to rescue Mary from captivity and marry her. In this he was supported by the Earls of Northumberland and Westmorland. Elizabeth discovered the plot, transferred Mary to Tutbury in Staffordshire under the protection of five hundred men, drove the northern earls over the Border, and imprisoned the Duke of Norfolk.

The next plot was much more ambitious. On 11th January, 1570 the Regent Moray was shot dead in Linlithgow's main street. He was succeeded by Darnley's father, the Earl of Lennox, who hated Mary more than any man alive. But just as Mary's chances of regaining power in Scotland looked gloomy, there came a chance for her to take the English throne. In May 1570 Pope

> "But she [Elizabeth] whose princely breast was touched near
> With piteous ruth of her [Mary's] so wretched plight,
> Though plain she saw by all, that she did hear,
> That she of death was guilty found by right,
> Yet would not let just vengeance on her light." *Edmund Spenser, The Faerie Queene, 1596.*

Opposite Thomas Howard, fourth Duke of Norfolk, at his trial for high treason in 1572. Although he had never met Mary, he wanted to marry her. He was executed for his part in the Ridolfi plot.

Pius V issued a Bull excommunicating Elizabeth I and releasing all English Catholics from their duties towards her. This raised the possibility of a mass Catholic rising on Mary's behalf. First, however, she would have to be freed.

At this point the Duke of Norfolk was released from the Tower of London on condition that he would have nothing more to do with Mary. Norfolk soon broke this agreement by joining a new plot being organized by Roberto Ridolfi, a London-based Florentine banker. The scheme, which was supported by a group of English Catholics, involved a Spanish invasion of England, the overthrow of Elizabeth and the marriage of the Duke of Norfolk to Mary, who would then become the new Queen of England. Unfortunately for Norfolk the plot was discovered. Although he had never met Mary and denied all knowledge of the Ridolfi plot, he was tried and executed on 2nd June, 1572. Many powerful Englishmen pleaded with Elizabeth to put Mary on trial for treason but the English Queen decided against such drastic action. She thought her own position was best served by keeping Mary alive but in captivity.

The Queen of Scots continued to dream of Spanish armadas and French fleets coming to her rescue, but neither Spain nor France felt inclined to go to war with England over Mary. They made promises but did nothing. So the years dragged on until 1585, when she was taken again to Tutbury and put under the custody of a new jailer, the fanatical Puritan Sir Amias Paulet. He detested everything Mary stood for and made it impossible for her to smuggle her letters out in the normal way. Paulet's vigilance enabled the government spymaster Sir Francis Walsingham to arrange a trap for Mary. When she was taken to new quarters at Chartley in December, Walsingham persuaded a local brewer to smuggle out Mary's letters in a beer barrel. Naturally Mary was delighted to take up the offer. In turn Walsingham was delighted at an arrangement which enabled him to intercept every letter that Mary sent. He kept copies of them all, and patiently waited for

Mary to become involved in yet another plot, so that he could pounce.

The next conspiracy was hatched by Sir Anthony Babington, a wealthy Catholic squire who had been Mary's page at Sheffield, where he had fallen under her spell. Now he convinced Philip II of Spain that if Elizabeth were murdered, English Catholics would rise up in support of Mary, and England could be conquered by Spain. Babington told Mary about the plot, and she wrote back agreeing to it. Every letter sent was copied by Walsingham, and by 11th August he had enough evidence to arrest Mary as she and Paulet left Chartley to take part in a hunt. Her papers were seized and she

Above The assassination of the Earl of Moray, Mary's half-brother and Regent of Scotland. He was shot dead in the main street of Linlithgow in 1570. Mary wore mourning for him, but arranged a pension for his assassin.

was taken to Tixall to await Elizabeth's decision. Babington himself was arrested three days after Mary and forced to confess all the details of the plot. One month later he was executed.

Mary had fallen into the trap laid down by Walsingham, but she had not acted innocently. She knew that Babington planned to assassinate Elizabeth, and felt that it was a fair price for her freedom. She had also allowed herself to agree to a foreign invasion of England in order that the Catholic religion could be restored by force. By any standards she had committed treason, even though she was not a subject of Elizabeth I. Years of imprisonment had made her impatient for her freedom, and in her haste she had been careless. At Sheffield she had woven the motto "In my end is my beginning" on a cloth of state. The Babington plot was the beginning of her physical end. Yet it also allowed her to die the death of a martyr rather than that of a prisoner.

Opposite In this engraving, Mary is swearing on the Bible that she has had no part in the Babington plot of 1586. One of her attendants is weeping, but Mary retains her dignity.

14 Trial and Execution

BY BECOMING INVOLVED in the plot to assassinate Elizabeth I, Mary had put herself into the hands of those who thought their world would be a safer place without her. She might argue that as an equal not a subject of the English Queen she was above the law, but as far as the English Government was concerned, she had committed treason in England. Under the Act of Association of 1585 "any person that shall or may pretend to the title to the Crown of this realm" could be executed if found guilty of conspiring against Elizabeth. On 25th September, 1586 Mary was taken to the ancient castle of Fotheringay in Northamptonshire, still under the watchful eye of Sir Amias Paulet, to await her trial. Now Cecil and his colleagues had Mary where they wanted her.

When approached by the English Commissioners, Mary claimed: "I do not recognize the laws of England." Only when told that her absence would not prevent the trial did she agree to appear, on condition that she was questioned on the single charge that she had planned the assassination of Elizabeth I. The two-day trial opened on Wednesday morning, 15th October and Mary, a victim of rheumatism, had to be helped in. She drew attention to the fact that she could no longer stand on her own two feet, saying: "My advancing age and bodily weakness both prevent me from wishing to resume the reins of government." Denying all knowledge of the Babington plot, Mary suggested that her only crime was to "have earnestly wished for liberty".

> **"Can I be responsible for the criminal projects of a few desperate men, which they planned without my knowledge or participation?"** *Mary Queen of Scots at her trial at Fotheringay, 15th October, 1586.*

Opposite Preparing for Mary's execution at Fotheringay Castle in 1586, from an old sketch.

These appeals for sympathy fell on the deaf ears of the Commissioners. They were convinced in advance of her guilt and had come to Fotheringay to condemn her. Feeling herself trapped, Mary complained to Cecil that he was determined to be her adversary. "I am the adversary to the adversaries of Queen Elizabeth," was Cecil's skilful reply. When her requests to appear before Parliament and to have a personal interview with Elizabeth were denied, Mary knew that her cause was lost. "My lords and gentlemen," she told the English Commissioners, "I place my cause in the hands of God." Unfortunately her cause was in the hands of the English Government, while her fate lay with Elizabeth.

At a meeting in the Star Chamber on 25th October, the Commissioners found Mary guilty of involvement "in matters tending to the death and destruction of the Queen of England". Both Houses of Parliament requested that Elizabeth I should authorize Mary's execution as "due punishment . . . for her most detestable and wicked offences". Instead of immediately granting this request, Elizabeth waited until 1st February, 1587 and even then had the death warrant placed among routine state papers so she might afterwards claim to have signed it by mistake.

Meanwhile, Mary was left to the tender mercies of Sir Amias Paulet who, as a convinced Puritan, wanted to humiliate the Catholic Queen of Scots into a feeling of guilt for her sins. He removed the royal canopy above her chair and told her: "No living person has ever been accused of crimes so frightful and odious as yours." Mary, now content to die as a martyr, was unconcerned. She replaced the canopy with a crucifix and told her jailer she was willing to die for her religion. Had Paulet been less of a religious man he might have helped her do just that, for Elizabeth asked him to "shorten the life" of the Queen of Scots to avoid the political embarrassment of an execution. An indignant Paulet refused by telling Elizabeth that he could not "make so foul a shipwreck of my conscience . . . to shed blood without law or warrant".

> **"You have planned in divers ways and manners to take my life and to ruin my kingdom by the shedding of blood."** *Elizabeth I to Mary, October 1586.*

Opposite Mary hears the news that she is to be executed.

So the execution went ahead on Wednesday, 8th February, 1587. In the early hours of the morning Mary wrote her last letter, to her brother-in-law Henry III of France, insisting: "The Catholic faith and the assertion of my God-given right to the English crown are the two issues on which I am condemned." Around 10 a.m. she appeared in the great hall of Fotheringay Castle and walked to the wooden stage on which the block had been placed. She wore a black satin dress with a white veil and carried her crucifix and prayer book. The Dean of Peterborough attempted to shake her Catholic faith but Mary calmly told him she had come to spend her blood for her religion.

After pardoning her executioner in advance Mary, helped by her lady-of-the-bedchamber Jane Kennedy, undressed down to a red petticoat. Jane Kennedy bound Mary's eyes before she knelt down to place her head on the block, where she repeated: "*In manus tuas, Domine, confide spiritum meum*" (Into your hands, O Lord, I commend my spirit). When the first axe-blow struck her head instead of her neck Mary was heard to mutter "Sweet Jesus". Even the second blow did not completely cut through her neck and a third was needed to separate the head from the body. When the executioner held up the head by the hair there was an unexpected thud: the grey-haired head fell from his hand leaving him holding an auburn wig. "So perish all the Queen's enemies," shouted the Dean of Peterborough. Though not quite. From underneath Mary's petticoat emerged her pet Skye terrier. It had sneaked into the great hall under the skirts. Now it would not leave the mutilated corpse of its mistress.

Opposite Mary in her petticoat blindfolded for her execution in 1586. She pardoned the executioner in advance.

15 Life after Death

WAS MARY QUEEN OF SCOTS a monster or a martyr? That is the question that has divided opinion down to our own day. As a young woman Mary had been treated like a goddess. After her marriage to Bothwell she was widely regarded as a criminal. George Buchanan, one of the greatest scholars in Europe, had read Latin to Mary at Holyrood, but when she fell from power he used his brilliance to poison the atmosphere against her. Mary called him a "vile atheist" but he had rather more to say about her. In 1571 his *A Detection of the Doings of Mary Queen of Scots* portrayed Mary as a monster who had planned the murder of Darnley so she could marry Bothwell. And that has remained the case against her.

It is now clear that Buchanan was wrong and Mary was not a criminal, but the victim of a conspiracy. Her half-brother Moray had put up a case against her to the English Commission because he was personally involved in the Riccio and Darnley murders. Her Secretary Maitland had tampered with the Casket Letters because he had personally urged Mary to get rid of Darnley. Her Chancellor Morton had produced the Casket Letters because of his own part in the murder of Darnley (for which he was eventually executed). These three men were simply acting in accordance with Elizabeth I's motto "strike or be stricken"—it was either Mary or them. As for Elizabeth, she sided with Moray, Maitland and Morton because that allowed her to get rid of the most dangerous rival to her throne.

Mary's fault, if it be a fault, was in marrying the man of her choice. Against the advice of those in power she

Opposite George Buchanan (1506–82) the scholar and Reformer. He became Mary's classical tutor in 1561 and dedicated his Latin version of the Psalms to her. After Darnley's death, he wrote an attack on Mary and became tutor to James VI.

Overleaf Pierre de Chàtelard, the French poet, serenading Mary.

Right Mary's pet dog discovering Pierre de Châtelard under her bed in 1562.

had married Darnley, and he was her downfall. In an age when queens needed superhuman calm, Mary wore her heart on her sleeve as well as a crown on her head. But since her execution she has enjoyed a life after death, shining through history like a brilliant star eclipsing her enemies. She has become a popular idol, the heroine of novels and plays and films.

Above all she has remained the darling of poets. As a young woman her beauty was hymned by Pierre de Ronsard. Another French poet even died for her. Pierre de Châtelard followed Mary to Scotland and became so infatuated with her that he hid under her bed. When he was executed in 1562 for this offence he died praising "the most beautiful and the most cruel princess of the world".

Since then countless other poets have lost their hearts

"**Look to your consciences and remember that the theatre of the world is wider than the realm of England.**" *Mary Queen of Scots before her trial at Fotheringay, 13th October, 1586.*

to her. Robert Burns wrote a lament in which he has the captive Queen say:

"I was the Queen o' bonnie France,
    Where happy I hae been;
Fu' lightly rase I in the morn,
    As blythe lay down at e'en:
And I'm the sov'reign of Scotland,
    And mony a traitor there;
Yet here I lie in foreign bands,
    And never-ending care."

However, in 1800 the great German dramatist Friedrich Schiller devoted a play, *Maria Stuart*, to showing how Mary's moral courage was more than equal to her captivity. The Victorian poet Algernon Charles Swinburne wrote three verse tragedies around Mary and a long love-poem to her. Even T S Eliot, the founder of modern English verse, ended the second of his *Four Quartets* (1940) with Mary's celebrated motto "In my end is my beginning."

Nor is there any sign of Mary losing her power to inspire poets. As recently as 1971 a young Scottish poet Jake Flower (in the magazine *Scotia*, No 22, October 1971) saw the Queen of Scots as a symbol for his country's struggle for freedom:

"Mary Stuart
 You broke the heart
    Of many many men.
 But you'd a frosty pow
 An' a sair-sunk brow
    Before they killed you, hen.
 The axe struck thrice
 And you called to Christ
    That Wednesday at ten.
 And I'll always see
 Till my country's free
    Them murder you again."

"More bright than stars or
    moons that vary,
Sun kindling heaven and hell,
Here, after all these years,
    Queen Mary,
    Farewell." *Algernon Charles Swinburne, Adieux à Marie Stuart, 1883.*

"In my end is my beginning."
Mary Queen of Scots, motto embroidered on royal cloth of state at Sheffield.

Principal Characters

Babington, Sir Anthony (1561–86). Wealthy English squire executed for plotting to assassinate Elizabeth I and make Mary Catholic Queen of England.

Beaton, Cardinal David (1494–1546). Pro-French Catholic opponent of Mary's proposed marriage to Henry VIII's son, he was assassinated at St Andrews three months after having the Reformer George Wishart burned to death.

Bothwell, James Hepburn, Earl of (1536–78). Hereditary Great Admiral of Scotland and Mary's third husband, he fled Scotland after defeat at Carberry Hill and died insane in a Danish prison.

Catherine de Medici (1519–89). Wife of Henry II and mother of Mary's first husband Francis II, she became Regent of France on Francis II's death and was responsible for the St Bartholomew's Day Massacre of Huguenots.

Cecil, William (1520–98). As English Secretary of State he persuaded Elizabeth I to support the Scottish Reformers in 1560 and later directed Elizabeth I's policy of detaining and finally executing Mary.

Châtelherault, James Hamilton, Duke of (and Earl of

Arran) (1515–75). Governor of Scotland and Mary's heir presumptive on James V's death, his conversion to a pro-French Catholic position in 1543 provoked Henry VIII's "rough wooing"; replaced as Regent by Mary of Guise in 1554 he joined the Lords of Congregation and became Regent on the death of Mary of Guise.

Darnley, Henry Stuart, Lord (1546–67). Mary's cousin and second husband, and after her in line to the English throne. His outrageous conduct made many enemies and led to his assassination at Kirk o'Field.

Elizabeth I (1533–1603). Mary's cousin and Queen of England. Her excommunication in 1570 led to the Babington plot to assassinate her and replace her by Mary, who was eventually executed for taking part.

Huntly, George Gordon, Earl of (1512–62). Scotland's most powerful Catholic noble, his control of the north-east was crushed by Mary in 1562.

James V (1513–42). Son of Margaret Tudor and James IV, Mary's father died six days after her birth, distressed at the defeat of the Scots by the English at Solway Moss.

James VI and I (1566–1625). Mary's son and infant King of Scotland on her forced abdication in 1567, he became King of England and Scotland on Elizabeth I's death.

Knox, John (1505–72). Leader of the Scottish Reformation whose public defiance of Mary did much to undermine her authority.

Lennox, Matthew Stuart, Earl of (1516–71). After Arran in line to the Scottish throne he married Henry VIII's niece and was exiled in 1545 for supporting the "rough wooing"; holding Mary responsible for the murder of his son Darnley he became Regent in 1570 and was killed in a raid the following year.

Maitland, William, of Lethington (1528–73). A political leader of the Reformation, he became Mary's Secretary of State; he married Mary Fleming in 1567, helped overthrow Mary at Carberry Hill, then tampered with the Casket Letters to imply Mary's guilt in the Darnley murder.

Mary of Guise (1515–60). James V's second wife and sister of the powerful Guise brothers under whose influence she placed her daughter Mary in 1548, she replaced Châtelherault as Scottish Regent in 1554 but was defeated by the Reformers.

Moray, Lord James Stewart, Earl of (1531–70). Illegitimate son of James V and Margaret Erskine, he persuaded his half-sister Mary to return to Scotland, rebelled against her marriages to Darnley and Bothwell, and became Regent on Mary's forced abdication.

Morton, James Douglas, Earl of (1525–81). A member of Mary's Privy Council, he fled to England after taking part in the Riccio murder and later helped defeat Mary at Langside; he became Regent in 1572 but was eventually executed for his part in the Darnley murder.

Norfolk, Thomas Howard, Duke of (1536–72). Premier duke of England, he was executed for his part in the

Ridolfi plot to bring Mary (whom he never met) to the English throne as his wife.

Philip II (1627–98), King of Catholic Spain, he decided against marriage between Mary and his heir Don Carlos; his long-expected Spanish Armada was sent to England only after Mary's execution.

Riccio, David (1533–66). An Italian musician who became Mary's French Secretary in 1561, he was violently taken from her at Holyrood to be murdered with the consent of Darnley.

Table of Dates

1542   24th November, Scots defeated by English at Solway Moss.

8th December, birth of Mary at Linlithgow Palace.

14th December, death of James V at Falkland Palace.

1543   1st July, Treaties of Greenwich arrange Mary's marriage to Henry VIII's son Edward.

8th September, Governor Arran converted to pro-French Catholic policy.

9th September, Coronation of Mary at Stirling Castle.

1544   May, Henry VIII begins "rough wooing" of Mary.

1547   10th September, Scots under Arran defeated by English at Pinkie Cleugh.

1548   7th July, Scottish Parliament arranges Mary's marriage to Dauphin Francis.

7th August, Mary sails for France.

1554   April, Mary of Guise replaces Châtelherault (formerly Arran) as Regent.

1558   24th April, Mary marries Dauphin Francis in Notre Dame de Paris.

17th November, death of "Bloody Mary" Tudor; Elizabeth becomes Queen of England.

1559   18th September, Francis II of France crowned at Rheims.

1560   March, Huguenot Conspiracy of Amboise.
        10th June, death of Mary of Guise in
            Edinburgh Castle.
        6th July, Treaty of Edinburgh removes
            French from Scotland.
        11th August, Scottish Parliament approves
            Protestant Confession of Faith.
        16th August, Scottish Parliament abolishes
            authority of Pope and prohibits Mass.
        6th December, death of Francis II; Catherine
            de Medici becomes Regent of France.
1561   April, Philip II of Spain decides against
            marriage of Mary to his heir Don Carlos.
        19th August, Mary arrives at Leith.
        24th August, Mary holds private Mass at
            Holyrood.
        31st August, John Knox denounces Mass and
            is summoned before Mary.
1562   11th August, Mary rides north to confront
            Huntly.
1563   December, Knox summoned before Mary on
            charge of treason and found not guilty.
1565   29th July, Mary marries Lord Darnley in
            Catholic ceremony at Holyrood.
        26th August, Mary and Darnley leave
            Edinburgh to confront Chaseabout Rebels.
        6th October, Moray flees to England.
1566   9th March, murder of Riccio at Holyrood.
        19th June, birth of James VI in Edinburgh
            Castle.
1567   10th February, Darnley strangled at Kirk
            o'Field.
        12th April, Bothwell tried for Darnley's
            murder and acquitted.
        24th April, Bothwell abducts Mary at Bridges
            of Almond.
        15th May, Mary marries Bothwell in
            Protestant ceremony at Holyrood.
        15th June, Mary and Bothwell submit to
            Confederate Lords at Carberry Hill.

17th June, Mary imprisoned in Lochleven Castle.

24th July, Mary forced to abdicate in favour of James VI; Moray becomes Regent.

1568   2nd May, Mary escapes from Lochleven.

13th May, Mary defeated by Moray at Langside.

16th May, Mary flees to England.

October, English Commission meets at York to consider Mary's part in Darnley murder.

1570   23rd January, Moray assassinated in Linlithgow; Lennox becomes Regent.

May, Elizabeth I excommunicated by Pope Pius V.

1572   2nd June, Norfolk executed for his part in Ridolfi plot.

24th August, Massacre of St Bartholomew's Day.

1573   May, Edinburgh Castle, held by Maitland for Mary, taken by Regent Morton.

1586   11th August, Mary arrested at Tixall for her part in Babington plot.

15th–16th October, trial of Mary at Fotheringay Castle.

1587   8th February, Mary executed at Fotheringay Castle.

1588   Defeat of Philip II's Spanish Armada.

1603   27th March, death of Elizabeth I; James VI becomes King of England.

Further Reading

The letters (AA) indicate advanced readership level, (A) indicates average.

Bingham, Madeleine, *Scotland Under Mary Stuart* (Allen and Unwin, 1971). An "account of everyday life" emphasizing the poverty and lawlessnesss of Scotland at the time of Mary. (A)

Davison, M H Armstrong, *The Casket Letters* (Vision Press, 1965). A "Solution to the Mystery of Mary Queen of Scots and the Murder of Lord Darnley" which finds Mary innocent and Maitland guilty of tampering with the casket documents. (AA)

Donaldson, Gordon, *The First Trial of Mary Queen of Scots* (Batsford, 1969). An examination of the English enquiry into the Darnley murder showing that Mary's life imprisonment was a political compromise between Elizabeth I and Regent Moray. (AA)

Cowan, Ian B, *The Enigma of Mary Stuart* (Gollancz, 1971). An anthology of various opinions of Mary from the sixteenth century to the present day. (A)

Fraser, Antonia, *Mary Queen of Scots* (Weidenfeld and Nicolson, 1969). A major biography that is always sympathetic to "Mary, with that soft heart, that horror of bloodshed, that inclination towards mercy". (A)

Knox, John, *The History of the Reformation of Religion in Scotland* (Andrew Melrose, 1905). Knox's classic history of the Reformation including detailed accounts of his five interviews with Mary. (AA)

MacGregor, Geddes, *The Thundering Scot* (Macmillan, 1958). A sympathetic portrait of John Knox which justifies his attitude towards Catholic queens. (A)

Mahon, R H, *The Tragedy of Kirk o' Field* (Cambridge University Press, 1930). Examines the events of 9th–10th February, 1567 in great detail and finds Mary innocent and Darnley a victim of his own gunpowder plot to seize the Scottish throne. (AA)

Phillips, James Emerson, *Images of a Queen* (University of California Press, 1964). A study of sixteenth century writing on Mary revealing a "battle of the books" as to whether she was a martyr or a monster. (AA)

Strong, Roy and Oman, Julia Trevelyan, *Mary Queen of Scots* (Secker and Warburg, 1972). Mainly visual presentation of Mary through illustrations of portraits, jewellery and embroidery. (A)

Swinburne, Algernon Charles, *Mary Stuart* (Chatto and Windus, 1899). Verse tragedy in five acts based on the Babington plot and Mary's trial and execution at Fotheringay. (A)